A Marvelous Time

Christmas poems for people just trying
to make it through the season

Kate Landers

Published by
Vulgar Scullery Maid Publishing, LLC
vulgarscullerymaid.com

© 2023 Kate Landers
katelanders.com

ISBN: 9781960151100

Scan this QR code to hear the
author read her poems.

For Lisa

Are You Worth My Fancy Bow?

I sit here debating on who's going to get it
The superior bow on top of their present
This eight-dollar wonder, the gift buckling under
The weight of my fanciest bow.

The bliss when I laid eyes upon it
Like hearing Shakespearean sonnets
Its beauty divine, the stars aligned
Rapture in aisle twenty-nine!

A MARVELOUS TIME

It was glossy and spongy and thick
I needed it like I need a...breadstick
My face all aglow, if you have one you know
Veneration of a beautiful bow.

Its perfect, voluptuous swoops
Glittery, scintillant scoops
The last of its kind, and now it was mine!
This object of flawless design.

It came in a box, not a bag
That's important - I DO mean to brag
A clear plastic case, atop a doily of lace
Worth every bit its price tag.

I twirled out of Walmart in glee
Holding my treasure gently,
On a mission to wrap all the new-purchased crap,
That goes 'neath a Christmas tree.

And now I sit here surrounded
By a veritable red-and-green mountain
Of presents galore! For, oh, there's more
Than ninety-six, last time I counted.

Only one of these shall get my bow
It's quite the decision, you know
Who is deserving, which present most worthy?
To whom will I this adornment bestow?

It must go to somebody special
Someone who also will revel
In the decoration I give, this transformative,
Life-changing, ravishing bow.

So now I really don't know
What should I do with this bow?
Is there anyone worth its beauty and girth?
The answer, I'm thinking, is No.

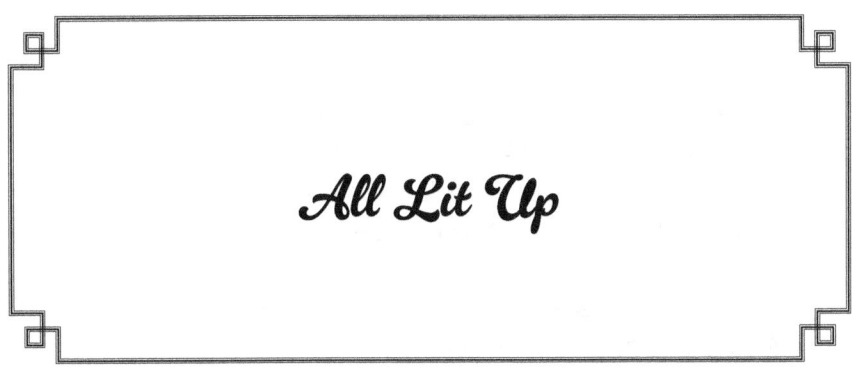

All Lit Up

It's the night before Christmas and all through my house,
Everyone's sleeping, including my spouse.
The stockings are hung but I gotta wrap shit,
So just like this tree, I'm about to get lit.

The kids passed out only an hour ago -
Time for me to play Santa: Ho-motherfucking-ho.
Grab the scissors, the tape, the bags and the bows,
A Coke and a glass, some ice and Old Crow.

The Christmas lights twinkle, and outside it's snowing.
How long will this take? I've no way of knowing.
How do other people wrap snow globes and bikes?
Dollhouses, baseballs, desk lamps and trikes?

Wait, where're the bows? I'll just accessorize that crap.
I'll soon be ready for a long winter's nap.
Voila. It's done. One present down.
I'm fuckin' awesome. Do we have any Crown?

Dang, that looks great. I'ma put some glitter on that now.
Maybe some googly eyes, too. Add some sequins and POW!
My son's going to love his new bike with all of this bling.
It's personalized with love – something Santa can't bring.

Aw, hell. We're out of whiskey. On to the scotch!
Watch me fill up these stockings – my skills are top notch!
Let's see, the baby gets a corkscrew, that's good.
And the wife can have this spare piece of wood.

Now what do I have in my pocket? Let's see –
A quarter, two dimes, and one green penny.
That's 25 cents for one kid and 21 cents for the other.
Well, I always did like my daughter a little
            bit more than her brother.

There now, I'm done! Peace out, Christmas Eve.
Won't my fam be impressed with all I've achieved?
The presents are done, and the stockings are, too.
Eating the cookie's the last thing to do.

Dang, that chocolate chip ain't tasting so good.
It don't want to be friends with the liquor, like I had
        hoped that it would.
Oh, God, I need to find a safe space and quick!
I tell you, it ain't easy being jolly old St. Nick.

The trashcan's too far; I need something now!
There's only one thing to do - Move aside, tree bough!
Ah, thank you, tree stand, even if you are filled with water.
The presents will hide everything – oh, hello there, daughter!

And son and dear wife - is it morning already?
Can't you people stop wobblin' and just hold steady?
And why's it so bright? And so loud? And so wet?
Hey, don't get mad! You ain't seen what I got for you yet!

Every growing girl needs a...a jock strap? That ain't right.
I must've gotten the gifts confused in the night.
Hey, come on! It's Jesus's birthday. Peace, joy, and forgive?
A little puke ain't a reason to be so combative.

Come on, family, let me buy y'all some waffles.
A trip to IHOP and we'll forget all our squaffles.
Squiffles, squabbles, you know what I mean.
Give your old dad a hug. And Happy Halloween!

Christmas Times Two

When your parents get divorced,
You might think it's sad
To choose whether you want to live
With your mom or dad

But if they share joint custody
And feel guilty they messed up
Well now you get two Christmases
So, kiddo, you're in luck

Twice the presents, twice the fun
No chores or obligations!
Just sit back and enjoy your first
Divorced kid vacation.

If your father was the type
To feed you cold oatmeal
Well no more, son, you're about to eat
A four-course breakfast meal

From scrambled eggs to sausage links
He'll be cooking all weekend
Gotta prove he's a better man
Than your mama's new boyfriend

And now it's all but a guarantee
That on Christmas Day you'll get
A roll of cash in your stocking
And probably a pet

A MARVELOUS TIME

And though you'll have to leave your pop
And go to mom's at four,
Remember that the day's not through
At mom's house there is more!

More candy canes, more chocolate
More presents 'neath the tree
Who knew divorce could be this great?
You've improved your family!

So spread the word to all your friends
Help them make up plans
To end their parents' marriages
I'm happy to lend a hand.

Here's my card, kid, with my number
I live right down the hall
I'm your friendly divorce lawyer
I look forward to your call.

A MARVELOUS TIME

Fleas Knob Heed Odd

Hola, Señor, bienvenidos!
And hola to all of your kids
Sus hijos y hijas y su esposa
Y todos sus grandkids!

¿Ustedes se sienten bien?
Me gusta escuchar that
Estoy aprendiendo a hablar español
But I bet you couldn't tell that

Lo se, lo se, I know I know
Hablo Spanish so well
Soy una americana
Pero quién puede to tell?

I just want to say to you
Y todo sus family
Espero que tiene a good Christmas
Or in Spanish - a Navidad feliz

Working Through the Holidays

Working through the holidays
Just me, myself, and I
Working through the holidays
'Cause I'm that type of guy

When the boss needs someone
To come on in
To brave the wind and snow again
They call on me, Reliable Jim,
'Cause I'm that type of guy

I never take a sick day
Even when I'm running hot
My throat is full of broken glass
My head is full of snot

I'm here at 8,
Don't leave till late
I never see the sun
And I probably won't get to pee
Until my shift is done

I haven't seen my coworkers
Since the week before Thanksgiving
Shame on them, that ain't the way
To make a decent living

You gotta be tough
To get ahead
Early to rise and late to bed
I'll get enough sleep
When I'm dead
(Which I hope happens soon - what?)

So here I sit all by myself
Making spreadsheets in Excel
Working hard on these accounts
Entering exact amounts
Giving clients their discounts
For the holidays

I've never been so busy
Though I'm filled with some disquiet
For I just noticed yesterday
This whole place is silent

I haven't got a phone call since
November 23rd
And it's now nearing the end of
The month of December

And I've come to realize,
Slowly, yes it's true
I didn't get my last paycheck -
Does that seem odd to you?

I think it's time I pause my work
And do a little digging
On what the heck has happened
Since the week before Thanksgiving

Ahh...

A Google search turns up info
About my company
It seems we filed for bankruptcy
...and nobody told me.

A MARVELOUS TIME

Good Advice

Cheers to all the people
Not friends or family
Who will still be getting gifts
From my wife and me

Here's to all you bastards
On the edges of our lives
The schmucks I know in passing
And your mediocre wives

I hardly even know you
Yet I cannot find a reason
That doesn't make me look like Scrooge
For stiffing you this season

So even though I know you
On a superficial level,
I'm giving you a gift so you
Don't think that I'm the devil

But since I do not know you
Or care just what you get
I've amassed a pile of goods,
Cheap and generic

Thus I grant them to you
My outer-circle friends
(Though really you're more like
Vague acquaintances)

Candles for my daughter's coach
A bath pouf for my vet,
Dish towels for the Home Room Mom
I've never even met

Snowglobes for my siblings
From my father's second wife
To the members of my carpool,
I'll bestow some new flashlights

A MARVELOUS TIME

Scented lotions for the men
Who clean my gutters on the weekends
And for the FedEx driver,
Some essential oily blends

Toothbrushes and Kleenex
For my second cousin's kids
Brew Your Own Home Beer kit
For my psychotherapist

For my long-time hairdresser,
A quesadilla press
A travel-grooming kit
For the new receptionist

Potholders and Chapstick
For the pastor of my church
For my coulrophobic colleague
A book on clown research

To my boss I'll give
A two buck, slightly-damaged windshield scraper
And to the barista at Starbucks -
A pack of toilet paper

To my geriatric neighbors
A glitter-making kit
And my postman shall receive
A brand new seat for his toilet

To the cashier at the grocery store,
I graciously bestow
A single roll of paper towels
And a slightly-used pillow.

To the trash collectors
Who have never missed a day
A coupon for a free dessert
At the Indian Buffet

If you are not sure this year
To whom to give a present
Let my poem guide you
And avoid any resentment

So when you go out shopping
For people on your list
Make sure to set aside some gifts
For assholes you have missed.

It's Christmas Time, You Assholes!

Driving around town just to see all the twinkles
From Christmas lights and all the happy peoples

Driving around town while bundled up tight
In my cozy wool coat this frosty winter night

So strictly speaking it's still autumn
And October has just begun

And technically it's 86 degrees
And all of the trees still have their stupid leaves

But even though schools have only just started
And summer only very recently departed

I know I'm not the only one
For whom the Christmas season has already begun

I shop for presents all year long
"The Little Drummer Boy" is my favorite song

I know all Santa's reindeers' names
I always smell like candy canes

And now I cannot hardly wait
Hurry Santa, don't be late!

But as I drive through my city
Something strange occurs to me

Everything looks exactly the same
Nothing's different, nothing's changed

I look in all the store windows
Where Christmas deco always goes

But all they got is ghosts and bats
Witches with their pointy hats

There's nothing fun about zombies,
Werewolves, monsters, or mummies

Where's the snowflakes and the trees?
Who gives a shit about Halloween?

Where's the Santa? Where's the snow?
Do goblins bring you presents? No!

Why's it seem that nobody's
Ready for Christmastime like me?

A MARVELOUS TIME

Where are all the carolers, strolling down the street?
I remember this time last year, it was Dickens's wet dream

The streetlamps were all wrapped up to look like candy canes
There was fake snow sprayed in every store
          fronts' frosted window panes

You could buy pictures with Santa on every street corner
I'ma find out what's going on - Hey you! Officer!

I demand to know with my rights as a citizen
When the city will let this year's Christmastime begin?

What do you mean it ain't up to you, or to the city?
It's up to all the citizens, individually?

I guess that means it's now my job to set these
          people straight
I'll have to do a PSA up and down the street.

Attention y'all, can I have your attention, please?
I need y'all to stop doing your thing,
          and start listening to me.

I'm going to need some cheer from y'all immediately
I wanna see the enthusiasm of Christmas previously

I want to see some reindeer gliding on rooftops
I want someone to fix me a drink with
          booze and cream, served hot!

I want to see a parade and people celebrating
I want to see whole families bust their ass ice skating

I want to see some middle-aged guy dressed like Buddy the Elf
I want to see generic stockings on every Walmart shelf

I want to feel that magic, that snuggly, cuddly, tingle
That only comes but once a year with a visit from Kris Kringle

I can't go another month without Christmas in my life
If I don't hear a carol soon, I think that I might die.

So come on people, help me. Help me to help you!
Don't you want to celebrate Christmas in fall, too?

What do you mean it's too hot out and you think you'd like to see
Halloween pass, the air turn crisp, and also Thanksgiving?

If we did all that, we'd still have to wait another two months or more!
All I'm asking is to see a little holiday cheer inside your store!

And on the streets, and in your homes, and in your cold, dead hearts
Christmas can't come three months early unless
          we ALL agree to start

But judging by how you're glaring at me, I get it, I do. I'll go.
But mark my words, just like Frosty, I'll be back with the first snow.

A MARVELOUS TIME

Kevin, the Absolute Worst Reindeer

Now way up there at the cold North Pole
Lives Santa and his elves and some other folks you know
Like Vixen and Blitzen, and Comet and Cupid,
All of the others, and Kevin, who's stupid.

He started off life just like any other
With a slow-witted father and an empty-headed mother
But before his antlers began to sprout
We learned just what young Kevin was about.

He never cared much for sports or schoolin'
Just watched the TV, a-sittin' and a-droolin'
He'd stay up late and sleep till four
Never helping with the dishes or any other chore.

As a teen he got into some trouble one day
When he and some friends "borrowed" Santa's sleigh
He probably would've gotten away with it, too
If it weren't for the video he put on YouTube.

Finally his parents had had quite enough
So they packed up Kevin and all of his stuff
Sent him to school for troubled young deer
Where Kevin lasted less than half of a year.

The next school was known for being sort of tough
While they taught reindeer all the different kind of stuff
They needed to know to get a job one day
Traveling round the world and pulling Santa's sleigh.

But when all of the reindeers was learning how to fly
Soaring off cliffs and climbing to the sky,
Kevin just laughed and was kind of a jerk
As he said, "Screw that! It's too much work!"

Well he flunked out of art and he flunked out of math
Never learned how to fly or how to read maps
But he earned a few D's, which allowed him to pass
So he graduated, dead-last in his class.

And that's pretty much just how it went
Till he landed a job in middle-management
Where he sits at a desk and grows real fat
As the North Pole's top-earning bureaucrat.

Well he got himself a wife named Mary-Eloise
And they do whatever they damn well please
Like leaving out pumpkins through the New Year
Or going to a barbecue and drinking all the beer.

They got two ugly kids named Snowy and Belle
Who like going to the workshop and heckling the elves.
They eat all of Mrs. Claus' fresh-baked cookies
Then chase the younger deer and give them noogies.

All of the neighbors hate the whole Kevin clan
And avoid them all just as best as they can
'Cause his cat leaves turds in their kid's sandbox
And his truck's always blocking their whole mailbox,

They don't lend him nothing that they expect back
And they don't trick-or-treat down his cul-de-sac.
When Santa comes through just to say Howdy-do,
He always avoids old you-know-who.

But Kevin don't mind 'cause Kevin don't know
'Cause Kevin's always been, well, kind of slow
So Kevin keeps doing whatever Kevin does
Like getting real drunk and firing his guns

Or going to the movies and talking real loud
Or farting while standing in the middle of a crowd
Leaving seats up when they should be down
Tossing cigarette butts on the ground.

Yep, Kevin is a reindeer no one likes
Just living his life in the cold Klondike
His chance of being famous is pretty slim
So that's why I had to write a poem about him.

Home for the Holidays

It's time to pack up our RV
And drive on down to Tennessee
The wife and the kids and the dogs and me
Heading back home to Tennessee

It's been ten years since we've come through
In that time we grew and grew
Not just the kids, we grown-ups too,
A li'l sideways, is how we grew

Going back home to Mama's house
Can't wait to see the old farmhouse
Gonna eat corn and brussel sprouts
Gonna show the kids the old farmhouse

Gonna take walks through the cornfield
Gonna pet the cows standing in the hayfield
Show the kids how a potato's peeled
Gonna step in shit in the hayfield

Gonna sleep in separate twin beds
'Cause that's all she has, Mama says
Gonna take a dump behind the shed
'Cause the plumbing's funny, Mama said

Gonna get up early to milk them cows
Gonna ask Mama to not smoke in the house
'Cause it bothers me, my kids, and spouse
"But," Mama says, "It ain't your house."

Gonna teach the kids to skin a deer
'Cause they're eating up all the corn around here
"I run 'em over with my John Deere,"
Says Mama, talking 'bout the deer 'round here

Gonna chop down a pine for Christmas Day
Gonna decorate a manger with real hay
Gonna cringe a little bit when I hear Mama say,
"Get your fucking dogs outta my hay!"

Gonna eat corn for the fifteenth time
Explain being liberal ain't a crime
Order some Xanax off Amazon Prime
Smoke some pot (which also ain't a crime)

Gonna say a blessing on Christmas Eve
For family and love and joy and peace
Gonna chase a squirrel out the Christmas tree
Gonna give up on joy and peace

Gonna eat corn instead of pancakes
When I come downstairs on Christmas Day
Gonna take a walk o'er the hills today
Try to not cry on Christmas Day

Gonna sit down for dinner tonight
Hoping everything will be alright
When there on the table I catch the sight
Of corn to my left, and corn to my right

Something snaps inside of me
And all of a sudden I can't see
Nothing but corn, not a thing
Little cob devils, is all I see

Sitting in this blinding light
Of yellow nuggets, pure and bright
As the sun, I just might
Lose my goddamned mind tonight

A MARVELOUS TIME

"Fuck this house and fuck your corn!
We're outta here first thing in the morn."
"You been in pain in my ass since the day you was born!"
Mama says, defending her corn

Early next morning 'round 6 AM
We're all in the RV again
The dogs and me and all my kin
Ready to hit the road again

Mama comes out still in her nightgown
"I'm sorry," she says with a little frown
"Come and see me next time you're around,
"Don't wait till I'm buried in the ground."

I tell her I love her as we start to leave
'Cause that's how it is in my family
We don't agree on everything,
But we stick together, my family

I slide behind the steering wheel
And look upon all those cornfields
I drive into the rising sun
And mow them stalks down, one by one.

Karen at the Mall

Look, my darlings! Just up ahead!
There's Santa, he's waiting for you!
When we get there, don't forget what I said:
Do exactly what I tell you to do.

Now Laura, you sit on Santa's right knee,
And Lewis, you're on the left,
Ok, look at me and smile 1-2-3!
Hey Santa, are you dumb or just deaf?

Smile, I said Smile, I said SMILE, Santa Claus!
I've got a good lawyer on speed-dial!
One push of this button is all it'll take
To sue your ass out of this mall!

You people relax. It ain't your turn yet!
And don't you dare roll your eyes at me.
You think after cuddling with my kids, he wants
Your butt-ugly child on his knee?

Come on, kids, we're done here, I'm tired, let's go!
Santa's not real anyway.
Oh, yeah, that's right. Didn't you know?
So sorry I ruined your day.

No, Lewis, that's not what I meant
I just meant that that Santa's a fake
The real Santa's waiting for the lord's advent,
So you better be good, for Chrissake!

A MARVELOUS TIME

Stop crying, Laura, I'll take your picture
Next to the Christmas tree!
But I swear to God, kids, if you don't move quicker
I'll tell Santa to skip Tennessee.

Sweet Jesus have mercy! Who told all the Pagans
To come out and worship THIS tree?
Who are all you people, just standing around?
The Hillbilly Bourgeoisie?

Move aside, people, get out of the way!
I just want a cute picture of my kids!
That's it, my two snowflakes, now smile big for Mommy,
Excuse me, did I just get spritzed?

Hey Kiosk Lady, I don't remember saying
I wanted to sample your stuff.
I don't care if you're just doing your job,
I'ma break that bottle and shove—

Hey! Watch it, people! Quit crowding around!
Ugh! There's candycane in my hair!
I don't care you're here for the All-Boys Choir
It sounds like they're murdering cats up there.

Oh, but it seems we got here at just the right time
For here comes their special guest!
He's lazy and rude with a bad attitude,
Who can it be? Can you guess?

It's Santa! It's Santa! The big, ugly jerk
Who makes children cry all day!
Hey Santa? Yeah, you remember me?
Here, have some Pumpkin Spice Latte!

A MARVELOUS TIME

Officer, Officer, you don't understand!
Those people are all telling lies!
No, I don't need to be escorted out,
I'll find my own way out of Satan's franchise!

That's it, kids, I'm over this holiday,
So listen up Laura and Lewis,
Commit every good memory you have of Christmas,
Because, babies, next year we're Jewish!

Christmas

Twinkly lights
And candy canes
Black Friday shoppers gone insane
Santa's coming
Ho Ho Ho!
Gatlinburg's phony snow

Extra presents
"Just in case"
Like nose-hair trimmers in a travel case
Or plaid potholders
From the dollar store
(I would've tried harder, if I liked you more)
Christmas cards
From distant relations
No one RSVP'd to
My invitations
Bake a chocolate yule time log
Recycle lots of catalogs
100-dollar Christmas trees
Harry & David salami and cheese
16 versions of Jingle Bells
Retail workers' personal hells

Christmas

Seasonal affective disorder
Delays with my on-line order
Why'd you give my kid a recorder?
Fresh-baked sticky buns

Secret Santas at the office
All my kids have streptococcus
Walmart's turned wild and lawless
For breakfast I had Tums.

18-hour family road trips
Red wine, grudges, and loose lips,
Recipe for apocalypse
Yeah, I gave your kid drums.

Christmas

Children snuggled in their beds,
Stocking up on headache meds.
Family photos, Christmas cards,
Maxing out the Mastercard.
Peppermint and gingerbread,
Sleeping on a blow-up bed.
"A Christmas Story" on TBS,
My whole house is a mess.
Santa's got a lot of stops,
Cocoa with a shot of Shnapps.
Eggnog, turkey, pumpkin pies,
Heading straight to my thighs.
Trying to make the Yuletide gay,
Growing colder every day.

Christmas.

Want to be naughty, but have to play nice,
Everything is Pumpkin Spice,
Snowflakes falling in the air,
Red Cross Santas everywhere,
Elf-on-a-Shelf is still a fad,
Gonna rat on you if you're bad.
Sadistic parents laughing 'cause
Their kid's terrified of Santa Claus.
Forgot the words to "Silent Night,"
"Somethin...somethin...somethin...bright?"
Kids snuck down and opened gifts,
'Cause they're impatient little shits.
Awkward office Christmas parties,
"Whose Xeroxed naked buttocks are these?"

Christmas

A MARVELOUS TIME

My kid only wants one thing this year
And that's one of Santa's flying reindeer.
I told her "Sure," just to avoid a fight,
I'll let my husband set that right.

Christmas

Fancy hand towels – folded twice,
Washcloth on top, so it looks nice.
Little snowmen made of soap,
But can you use them? Mm-mm, nope!
Potpourri and candles, too,
To cover up your smelly poos.
A Frosty trashcan, a Santa rug,
A toothbrush in a festive mug!
Candy-cane scented toilet paper,
Kind of weird now, but you'll thank me later.

Christmas.

Half my family is divorced,
And my husband's family, too
So we celebrate two times four
(Or is it four times two?)

I spend the day driving around
From county to county and town to town
Trying to turn my frown upside down
And delay my mental breakdown.

Christmas

My gingerbread house
Turned into a Graham Cracker Shack
When the chimney fell off
And the roof got cracked.

King's Icing just wouldn't do,
So I had to use Gorilla Glue.
Warned the kids, I said, "Don't eat it!"
They heard my advice, but did they heed it?

'Course not.

Everything worked out ok in the end,
The kids are all alright,
And with their lips glued tight together,
It's been one Holy Silent Night.

Christmas

As this list draws to a close
I'll quickly mention all of those
Other things I haven't yet
It's Christmastime! Let's not forget:

A MARVELOUS TIME

Jingly bells
And apple cider,
Christmas trees
Catching fire.
Wrapping paper,
Stick-on bows.
My waitress and her
Runny nose.
Building snowmen in the sun
A new flu season has begun.
Making family memories
Forgot to pack spare batteries.
TV Specials, Hallmark movies,
Passing out in my jacuzzi,
Brownies, cookies, fudge galore,
Checkout lines out the door,
Working extra double shifts.
Forgot to label all my gifts.
Million-Light Enchanted Gardens,
Slipped while taking out the garbage.
Snow Days and Christmas pageants!
Best Buy has a lot of "gadgets."
Getting gift cards for my teen,
So he can buy some more ripped jeans.
Scottie dogs and mistletoe,
Wishing I could be in Rio...
sigh

On the 26th I'll be sad it's over,
Can't wait till the season starts again
         – next October.

That Christian Life

Now Christmas is for celebrating
That one special guy
Who swooped to Earth on angels' wings,
Descended from the sky

He came to save us all
By forgiving all our sins
But I bet he woulda given up
If he'd'a met my kids

The good Lord taught us all
Peace and love and grace
But he didn't have a two-year old
Spit cider in his face

I doubt he ever had to clean
Up 16 rolls of tape
Zig-zagged all across the room
"So Santa can't escape"

I doubt he had a fruitless search
All through his pantry
For the 97 gingersnaps
His children ate last week

And I don't think I can picture him
Trying to wrap some gifts
With children sliding 'neath the door
Additions to their lists

A MARVELOUS TIME

Or breaking half the ornaments
On his Christmas tree
The heirloom ones, passed down for years
Through his family

I have a hard time picturing
What was in his stocking
But I bet when he reached his hand in
He didn't hear it squawking

And I bet his family let him sleep
Til late on his birthday
Instead of screeching 'fore sunrise,
"Get up! It's Christmas Day!"

So on that day in December
When we're honoring our king
Forgive me if I seem put out
When my children want something

I know I could provide them more
But if they even ask
I'll say, "Pucker up your lips, children
And kiss my fucking ass."

What Christmas is Really About

I think we can all agree that somewhere along the way
We lost sight of the true meaning behind Christmas Day

'Cause Christmas isn't about consumerism or anything tangible
It's really just a feeling you get, when your heart is full

Christmas time's for sharing, caring, love, and gratitude
And it's time for Instagramming all of your food

A MARVELOUS TIME

It's about trending hashtags and snowflake Snapchat filters
Flaunting your lifestyle to your ex-sorority sisters

It's taking twelve selfies with a Starbucks whipped cream mustache
(But it only took you one try, if anyone should ask)

It's dressing up your daughter in that dress with all the lace
Then letting her cry on Santa's lap till she's purple in the face

It's about going down to Target and buying seven trees
Of all the colors of the rainbow (hashtag diversity)

It's about gathering up your clothes for the local Goodwill store
The ones with all those stains and holes that you don't wear anymore

It's about getting creative with the Elf upon a shelf
And posting pictures in your Mom group before anybody else

It's about getting your nails done to look like little trees
It's about making TikTok videos at holiday parties

It's about matching outfits when you're getting portraits done
For your husband and your daughter (but not your new stepson)

A perfect gingerbread house with a little ginger man
(But after you post pictures, they'll go in the garbage can)

So if you want to prove that you are filled with Christmas spirit
Then grab a camera, hit record, and document that shit

Santa in a Swimsuit

Driving to the Walmart store
Gonna get my shopping done
Swimsuit, sunscreen, inner tubes,
So I can have some fun

Walk inside the Walmart store
On a sunny summer day
Checkin' my deodorant
'Cause I am real sweat-ay

Walking 'round the Walmart store
When what now do I see?
Santa and his eight reindeer
Staring back at me

I pause before this bright display
Of untimely Christmas cheer
Christmastime's a season, damnit,
Not the whole dang year!

Santa's busy, anyway,
Making all the toys!
Just because it's summertime
Don't mean he's unemployed!

He don't need to be here
And neither does this elf
Why is there fake snow already
Spread upon the shelf?

A MARVELOUS TIME

There's visions of the North Pole
As far as I can see
What the hell is going on
In Aisles 1, 2, and 3?

Outside Walmart's sliding doors
It's a hundred degrees
But once you round the swimsuit aisle,
THERE'S FUCKING CHRISTMAS TREES!

And mistletoe, and Christmas lights,
And artificial mantles
Wrapping paper, Christmas wreaths,
10,000 stupid candles

There's peppermint and gingerbread
And pumpkin spice galore!
I think that I may light a few
BURN DOWN THIS FUCKING STORE!

Alright, I'll go, I've said my peace
I won't bother you no more
Just let me buy these 99 items
That I came here for.

The Cheeriest Elf at the South Pole

My name's Twink and I'm an elf
And I live here all by myself
Working hard to make bad toys
For naughty little girls and boys

Santa sent me here last year
'Cause I don't have no Christmas cheer
I wear black and I'm no fun
And I bother everyone

When they sing carols, I just sigh
Don't ask me to smile, I'd rather die
I don't like cookies or cocoa
Or building snowman in the snow

So when Santa came to me one day
I wasn't shocked to hear him say
I don't exactly right fit in
With all my cheery elvin kin

He said that due to Global Warming
He had some greener ideas forming
He would not punish kids with coal
And he sent me down to the South Pole

He gave to me my own workshop
On a frozen, bleak hilltop
Far away from everyone
Where I will never see the sun

A MARVELOUS TIME

Where nothing grows and nothing lives
Except some stupid fat penguins
He gave me lumber, nails, and glue
Then waved good-bye and away he flew

He never asks if I'm okay
With being sent so far away
But I don't really mind at all
'Cause now I get to make beach balls

That pop the first time you use them
And gum textured like clotted phlegm

Teddy bears made from sandpaper
Chocolate-covered peas and capers

Toy airplanes made out of rocks
Splinter-covered wooden blocks

Ugly dolls and unicorns
With stubby, crusty, smelly horns

Play makeup that gives you rashes
Glitter made from Grandpa's ashes

Books where everybody dies
Socks, and shoes, and school supplies

When I lived in Christmas Town
I was the saddest elf around

But since I got moved down to here
I finally feel that Christmas cheer.

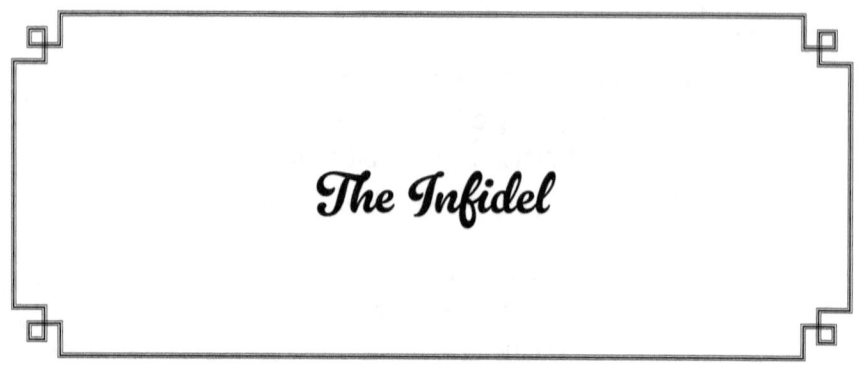

The Infidel

It was Christmastime at Hanukkah; there was Kwanzaa in the air
There were Santas, crosses, dreidels, and kinaras everywhere
There were over-crowded malls,
There was ham and matzo balls,
And then there was the Atheist.

No Christmas song or Kwanzaa drum could loose this sinner's spine,
Although she did partake of the eggnog and the mulled wine,
When revelers would start to sing,
And Christians cried, "Here comes the King!"
It was awkward 'round the Atheist.

She didn't make potato latkes or chocolate yuletide logs
She didn't care to go to church or to synagogue,
She didn't kneel on prayer mats
Or say a blessing for a lamp,
Because...duh.

She never cared to grab a deal by shopping on Black Fridays
She sang no songs of miracles or riding upon bobsleighs,
She'd never made a snow angel
Or even licked an icicle
But that's 'cause she was from the South.

Although she'd grown up cinched up tight within the Bible Belt
The spirit of the holidays she'd really never felt,
Especially on Friday nights
When getting left off fun invites
By people saying,
      "...Well, I didn't think an Atheist would want to come."

Her co-workers requested off December all through New Year's,
Knowing she, the Atheist, would surely volunteer
For clearly she, the nonbeliever,
Childless, single, free of fever,
Had nothing better to do with her life.

And so they gather after-hours and upon the weekends
Family, neighbors, co-workers, acquaintances, and friends,
Eating, drinking, singing, praying,
Giving presents, celebrating,
But not one moment contemplating
That one with no religion.

When her shift has ended every evening about ten,
She shuffles through the swirling cold into her old Datsun
She drives past stores and Christmas trees
Past carolers and bright marquees,
To wherever it is Atheists go.

Joyless, soulless, windowless beige-y, drab apartments
Or to wait in line for fun at Motor Vehicle Departments,
Or perhaps she's off to spoil the joy
For Christian girls and Jewish boys
By spreading 'round her nihilistic views.

No one knows just what to do with this godless heathen
How can Atheists participate throughout the holy season?
Should they celebrate that Festivus
The holiday for the rest of us?
Maybe a generic "Happy Holidays" will do.

The Offense

I can see it in your eyes
The way they sparkle, the way they dance
Your lips are twitching upwards,
And I can tell with just a glance

You're trying hard to hold it in,
Those blushing cheeks, that dopey grin
You've fucking gone and done it again.

You've bought me a Christmas present.

We are only office co-workers,
Nothing less, nothing more
That's why I give you shit
That I buy from the dollar store

Your cloying little teasers
As we pass by in the hall,
"Uh-oh, Santa's coming soon!"
Are not cute at all.

I dread the day you show up wearing
Your jingle jangle hat
And that stupid, ugly sweater
Featuring the Christmas Cat.

My coffee breaks have now become
Few and far between
As I try to slip out of the room
Without my being seen

You seem to take great pleasure
In forcing me to guess
What gift it is you're giving me
The Wednesday after next.

But I don't give a shit.

Finally the day arrives
I pull your present from my drawer
Where I chucked it after lunch
Only the day before

Knowing it's a lousy gift,
But still something to give
And now the onus is on you
To seem appreciative.

A MARVELOUS TIME

As usual, you've given me
Things I can do without -
A basket of stale potpourri
And a "rainfall" shower spout.

I don't even want these stupid things
But now I'm obligated
To gift you back and close this hellish
Loop you have created.

So here you go, you office fiend
You dog, you goon, you imp
Enjoy these expired mints,
And a coupon for some shrimp.

Yep! That's all you get, you slut!
"Wrapped" in a grocery bag!
I'm not wasting bows on you,
You horrible holiday hag!

This year please just take the hint,
You jolly old Saint Brick
I'm passive-aggressively begging you
Please don't be this thick!

Don't make me say it outloud,
I'm not a grinch, it's true!
It's just that I don't particularly
Like, know, enjoy, appreciate, need,
        want, regard, think about,
        care for, or respect you.

Mall Santa Blues

Son, I know your mama said she was just going to pop
Over there for a second into that shop,
But unless I can find that worthless mall cop,
It looks like you're stuck with me for a while.

But Santa don't get paid for babysitting
And it's 6 o'clock – time for quitting
Yet here I am, your caregiver unwitting
So let me unload on you while we wait.

I've been Santa Claus for 52 winters
Almost as long as I can remember
And I'm starting to dread each December
When Christmas time draws near.

See things are different now from when I started
Seems people and civility have long since parted
Why just today at least 12 children farted
While sitting on my lap.

Nine of 'em tried to pull off my beard
Some teenagers laughed and called me weird,
Son, I hate to say it, but I fear
It ain't fun being Santa anymore.

Each year the kids get a little more sassy
Department store elves get a little more brassy
While I'm left feeling a little less chatty
Some days I don't utter a single "Ho."

A MARVELOUS TIME

Every day I sit here on my throne
Waiting for people to get off their phone
So I can take a picture with little Jimmy and Joan,
While their parents just scroll away.

They want the Likes, not the memories
Nobody's paying any attention to me
So I've started secretly
Flippin' them the bird.

But what's worse is when the parents start laughing
And the lookie-loos begin clapping
And my dumbass assistant keeps photographing
When the children begin to cry.

See Santa gets no joy from children's misery
But some parents do, that's plain to see,
This season I've suffered four testicular injuries
From children trying to run away.

My boss this year is half my age,
I'm barely pulling minimum wage,
And my 5 minute smoke breaks cannot assuage
The pain of disappointment anymore.

Oh, I've got the Mall Santa Blues
And I know just what I'm going to do,
I'm going to dig this flask out of my boot
And drink away my Mall Santa Blues.

See, peppermint schnapps keeps Santa's beard white,
Keeps my cheeks rosy, keeps my eyes bright.
Keeps Santa from looking how he feels on the inside,
Like a zombie, shufflin' from his grave.

Now don't you go feeling sorry for me,
I've got 52 years of good memories,
And hey – no one looks better in fur trim than me,
'Cause I'm hootie-hootin' Santa Claus.

If only Mrs. Claus had seen it that way
Maybe I could've convinced her to stay,
Now it's just me and the reindeer, but hey –
I got all the toys.

Some days I just putter around,
Drive up through the mountains or across town,
Lately I've been thinking about moving down,
Like to San Andrés, where Christmastime's in summer.

Can't you just see me now?
Sipping on rum and curacao,
Sunburnt cheeks and a sweaty brow,
No malls for miles around.

Maybe next year I'll get out of this place,
Sell this suit and shave my face,
Take nothing that won't fit in my suitcase,
Drive the sled south as far as it'll go.

Between you and me, that sounds like a plan.
I can already smell the rattan.
Santa's bowlful of jelly is going to get tan,
Just as soon as I get out of this place.

Son, I see your mama is heading our way.
You'll be gone soon, so I'd just like to say,
I wish you the merriest of all Christmas Days,
Thanks for listening to a Mall Santa's blues.

What I Really Want for Christmas

What I want for Christmas
       cannot fit beneath a tree
I don't want cash or chocolate,
       fancy trips or gold jewelry
If I'm being truly honest with myself
       and all of you,
Here is what I want to make my
       Christmas dreams come true:

A mystery as to where my
       children actually are
'Cause judging by this trail of crumbs,
       they are not very far

A spouse that won't complain about
       my cauliflower rice
Botox in my lips, my cheeks,
       and right between my eyes

A MARVELOUS TIME

A son who sees the perfection in vacuuming my way,
A house that shrinks to dorm-room size upon cleaning day

Someone to water my plants, or steal them, I don't care
Someone to extract this gumwad from my daughter's hair

Self-resealing chip bags and rice pudding carton lids
So I can cut down on the food that's wasted by my kids

A backseat free from stickers, crumbs, crayons,
          straws, and boogers,
The ability to not gain weight from single grains of sugar

Someone who will dust my fans and pick up that hair tie
The one that I have stepped right over
          at least a thousand times

Someone who will use these coupons that shall soon expire
A bra that will not jab my armpit with its underwire

Someone who will sew this button back upon my blouse
A whole Christmas where no one eats the mints
          off my bread house

And so I fling these joyful wishes to the winter air
Hoping one may stick and grow and come to life somewhere

To all the parents out there, and also those sans kids
Those with hectic lifestyles living in unclean houses

May all your wildest hopes and dreams for
          the holidays come true
This is my last Christmas wish, and I'm giving it to you.

A Marvelous Time

"I'm hosting a party, December the 9th,
At exactly a quarter to eight.
I'll have oysters, fois gras, and of course caviar,
It's black tie, and please don't be late."

Such simple instructions, printed so clearly,
On the invites I sent out last week.
Show up, have some food, drink some wine, have a chat,
A marvelous time, don't you think?

So I polished the silver and ironed the linens,
And steam-cleaned the drapes and the rugs,
Washed all the china, dusted the cabinets,
And hid all my stained coffee mugs.

Bought new toilet paper (the good kind with lotion)
And six pounds of fresh potpourri,
A gold chandelier, a coatrack of bronze,
And a 19-foot Christmas tree.

It was then that I realized it wouldn't be a party
Without a nice fire a-blazing,
So I had a chimney installed early this week,
And now it looks just amazing.

But the light from the fire made my furniture look
Ever so slightly bland,
So this Wednesday I shopped for a new set of couches
And tables and chairs much more grand.

But when they arrived and the old was tossed out,
To my horror it was then that I saw,
That all my new furniture totally clashed
With the artwork and paint on my wall!

No time to shop for new paintings,
I decided there must be a way to get by.
Perhaps if I added a bit more turquoise
To Afremov's Burning Sky...

And that Lichtenstein really just needed
Some green, and some blue, perhaps black?
That's perfect! Now on to the Pollock!
Oh, I can drip better than that!

Now what a shame! An unfortunate mess!
It seems I forgot the drop cloth.
For there's paint everywhere – on the couch, in my hair,
Damn you, you sticky high-gloss!

Didn't I read once that polish remover
Will take care of all sorts of stains?
Let's give it a go, tip it up, there's the splash,
Now why is my couch in flames?

Oh I see a few embers flew out of the flue,
Which I guess I forgot to open,
There's smoke everywhere and it's burning my eyes,
But my circumstance isn't yet hopeless!

There's a fire extinguisher back in the closet
Behind all those wrapped Christmas presents.
I'll just pull them out all out, and the mop and broom, too,
Oh, that's where that TV set went!

And look at these boxes! And old record albums!
And photos and yearbooks and more!
My old winter coat! My crock-pot! My candles!
Now what was I looking for?

Well, it can't be important, whatever it was,
Or I surely would have remembered.
I'm just happy I opened this door and found
All of my long-lost treasures!

But before I even try and begin
To clean up all of this mess,
There is something I feel that needs my attention...
What was it? What was it? Oh yes!

The name cards! Dear me, how silly I am
To forget such an important thing!
Where do I keep those gilded note cards?
Oh, right! Near the napkin rings.

A MARVELOUS TIME

And speaking of rings, I haven't yet chosen
The theme of my dinner place settings.
And how can I choose such a thing for my guests
Before I know what they're getting?

Let's see, we'll have goose and slow-roasted duck,
Turnips and aged caviar,
Fried oysters, risotto, perhaps some charred greens,
And my specialty, pickled fois gras.

My friends all hire a caterer,
Whenever they throw a big party,
But not me; I stay calm as I cook enough food
To feed the United States Army.

Dash of this, pinch of that, now rub it all in
As I preheat the oven to bake.
Oops, forgot I needed to marinade that,
Now how long does it all take?

Four hours? Oh no! How can that be?
It's already nearing six thirty!
I wonder if things would move a bit faster
If I tripled these nine recipes?

No time to measure, just dump it all in,
It'll all taste fine, I'm sure.
A cup of salt, a liter of butter,
A half-gal of white vinegar.

Mix it together and bake at 400
For 45 minutes or so.
Or was it 500 for 20 to 30?
Where did that recipe go?

Ugh, there it is, 'neath some sticky mess
Well, it surely can't help me out now.
But I won't fret at all, for I don't need a book
To tell me what, when, or how.

La dee dum, la dee dee, and tra-la-la-la
As I mix, blend, stir, fold, and pour,
Damn! I forgot the lid to the blender,
Now the shit's all on the floor.

What more could go wrong? Is there anything else
That I should try to remember?
Ding Dong. Oh, god, don't tell me they're here
On this unholy night in December?

Is it really that time? Really, already?
Oh, god, don't tell me it's true.
Ding Dong. "I'm coming!" Oh, hell! Oh, crap!
Now what do I, what do I do?

Ding Dong Ding Dong! "I'm coming, you assholes!"
I swear some folks have no manners!
I smooth my hair back, wipe the tears from my eyes,
And smile wide just as I answer.

"Well hello! Do come in! You're all right on time,
You'll have to pardon the mess,
I've been cleaning and prepping all day for you,
And as you can see, I'm not dressed.

Please help yourself to – no, wait, it's not ready,
And damn! I forgot to buy wine.
I can offer you water and salted Ritz crackers,
That smell is just liver in brine.

A MARVELOUS TIME

Oh, that smell? Hm, I don't know,
Yes, it is rather pungent and smoky.
A mix of leather, fresh paint, polyester, and down,
It's plastic-y, acrid, and oak-y.

No, please, don't go yet! I've worked so hard!
I'll have these flames out in a jif!
And then we can all sit and relax,
The food'll be done in a bit!

Just try not to sit on this end of the couch,
Or on the tables and chairs,
And the paintings are wet, and so are the walls,
So I wouldn't lean back over there.

But please help yourself to all of my fine
Scented, three-ply toilet paper,
Does anyone, anyone need to go poop?
No? Well perhaps maybe later.

And I couldn't help notice that no one has yet
Removed their nice hats, coats, or gloves,
I bought a new coatrack, just for that purpose,
And this new chandelier just above.

Look at it! Look at it now!
Tell me how awesome it is!
Tell me you love it! It's the best that you've seen!
Or I'll kill you, your dogs, and your kids!

You bastards just sit there with no appreciation
For the trouble I've gone through today!
With your ugly, dumb faces and vacant-eyed stares,
Just look at yourselves, okay?

You with your bow tie, like a wooden lap dummy
And you with your hair up in braids!
Your long silky dress and your custom-fit suit!
You drive me completely insane!

A MARVELOUS TIME

Get out! Get out! Get out of my house!
Good-bye, good-night, and good-riddance!
I'll see you in hell, if I see you again,
Farewell! Fuck you all! Merry Christmas!

About the Author

Kate Landers lives in the southeastern United States where it rarely snows, which is just fine by her. She prefers fake Christmas trees over real ones, and her favorite Christmas movies are Home Alone (the original AND the sequel), and Bad Santa. Her favorite Christmas album is Mr. Hankey's Christmas Classics.

You can read more of her stuff at KateLanders.com, and find her other humorous book **I Pooped and It Was Amazing** at vulgarscullerymaid.com.

Scan this QR code to hear the author read her poems.

www.ingramcontent.com/pod-product-compliance
Lightning Source LLC
Chambersburg PA
CBHW070936120626
46546CB00004B/1432